ANCIENT EGYPT

by Pamela Dell

Content Adviser:
Jennifer Houser Wegner, PhD
Associate Curator
Egyptian Section, Penn Museum
University of Pennsylvania

COMPASS POINT BOOKS
a capstone imprint

Compass Point Books
1710 Roe Crest Drive
North Mankato, MN 56003
www.capstonepub.com

Editor: Anthony Wacholtz
Designers: Heidi Thompson and Lori Bye
Media Researcher: Eric Gohl
Library Consultant: Kathleen Baxter
Production Specialist: Laura Manthe

Image Credits
Alamy: Montagu Images, 38, North Wind Picture Archives, 27; BigStockPhoto.com: Juriah, 37;
Bridgeman Art Library: Ancient Art and Architecture Collection Ltd., 43, Private Collection/Stanton,
Charles R., 42; Corbis: Blue Lantern Studio, 35, Christie's Images, 26, Gian Berto Vanni, 24, Gianni
Dagli Orti, 20, National Geographic Society, 12, 29, 40, Sandro Vannini, 21; Newscom: akg-images,
41, akg-images/Franois Gunet, 31, 34, akg-images/James Morris, 18, akg-images/Werner Forman, 16,
Danita Delimont Photography/DanitaDelimont.com/Kenneth Garrett, 10, 32, Reuters/Handout, 33;
Shutterstock: Alperium, 5, BasPhoto, 15, bumihills, 13, Efremova Irina, 7, Mariia Sats, 11, Maugli,
cover (top right), Rachelle Burnside, cover (bottom left), sculpies, 4, Tee Scott, cover (bottom right),
valex61, 6, Vladimir Korostyshevskiy, 23; Wikipedia: Captmondo, 36, Jeff Dahl, 8, Public Domain, 9

Design Elements: Shutterstock: LeshaBu, MADDRAT, renew studio

Library of Congress Cataloging-in-Publication Data
Dell, Pamela.
  Ancient Egypt / by Pamela Dell.
    p. cm.
  Includes bibliographical references and index.
  ISBN 978-0-7565-4563-5 (library binding)
  ISBN 978-0-7565-4566-6 (paperback)
  ISBN 978-0-7565-4624-3 (ebook PDF)
  1. Egypt—History—To 332 B.C.—Juvenile literature.
  2. Egypt—Social life and customs—To 332 B.C.—Juvenile literature. I. Title.
  DT83.D43 2013
  932.01—dc23   2012007338

Editor's Note: Compass Point Books uses new abbreviations to distinguish
time periods. For ancient times, instead of BC, we use BCE, which means
before the common era. BC means before Christ. Similarly, we use CE,
which means in the common era, instead of AD. The abbreviation AD
stands for the Latin phrase *anno Domini*, which means in the year of our
Lord, referring to Jesus Christ.

Printed in the United States of America in Stevens Point, Wisconsin.
032012   006678WZF12

Table of
CONTENTS

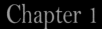

Chapter 1

Ancient Days

Beneath Egypt's scorching deserts lie the remains of a wondrous ancient civilization. While much has already been discovered of this unique culture, Egyptologists believe that many more mysteries and treasures are still buried in the sand. Huge temples and tombs, striking pyramids, the iconic Sphinx,

and giant obelisks inscribed with writings provide details from the distant past. Archaeologists have also unearthed the mummified remains of kings, queens, common people, and pets. They have found jewelry, vessels, paintings, weapons, and much more.

These findings tell the fascinating tale of the ancient Egyptian empire, a civilization that lasted thousands of years. In 3200 BCE Egypt was essentially two separate kingdoms. One was situated in northern Egypt, the other in the south. The kingdoms struggled against each other to gain entire control of the region. Finally, in about 3100 BCE, the southern kingdom claimed victory and the two merged into one.

From that point on, the ancient Egyptian culture evolved into one of the most incredible and complex civilizations ever to exist. It also lasted longer than any other human civilization. It thrived on the banks of the mighty Nile River for about 3,000 years. The civilization remained essentially the same until around 30 BCE. Then control of the land fell to a series of Roman emperors.

The pyramids at Giza (left) are distinct icons of ancient Egypt.
Stories from that time were recorded in hieroglyphs (above).

The Great Sphinx

The Egyptians are especially known for their stone sculptures called sphinxes. The most famous of these, the Great Sphinx of Giza, has intrigued the world for centuries. The fantastic sculpture has a human head and wears the headdress of a pharaoh. Carved from limestone, the Sphinx is the largest and oldest known statue of its kind in the world.

The Great Sphinx of Giza is about 200 feet (60 meters) long and 80 feet (24 m) tall.

Through Egypt's vast desert terrain, the Nile River flows like lifeblood. As it floods its banks every year, it waters a ribbon of rich land on either side. Just like today, life in ancient Egypt was centered in these regions. The ancient Egyptians called the area the Black Land, describing the fertile farmlands the Nile provided. The annual flooding of the river, known as the "Inundation," irrigated the crops and enriched the soil, making life possible.

Beyond the Black Land was the Red Land. The name described the miles and miles of hostile desert that stretched both east and west of the river. The deserts to the east were harsh and mountainous. They contained a network of dry riverbeds called wadis. The desert to the west was flatter, but just as dangerous.

In the north the Nile broke into many branches and emptied into the Mediterranean Sea. Traveling in this area of marshy land was not easy. To Egypt's south lay the land of Nubia. But here the river held a series of

The Nile River stretches 4,132 miles (6,650 kilometers) across northeastern Africa.

Upper Egypt, Lower Egypt, and the Nile

The shape of the Nile River is often compared to a lotus, a flower sacred to the ancient Egyptians. Look at the Nile on a map and you will see why. Its long, graceful "stem" curves northward through the land. Then, as the river reaches the Mediterranean Sea, it branches out, as if blossoming into many petals.

This beautifully shaped river begins deep inside the African continent. Once it enters Egypt, it travels first through the region the ancient Egyptians called Upper Egypt. As it flows from south to north, it reaches Lower Egypt and the marshy delta area.

The fact that Upper Egypt is in the south and Lower Egypt in the north sometimes confuses people. But it has to do with the terrain. Upper Egypt is situated on higher ground. Lower Egypt, the delta region, is much closer to sea level.

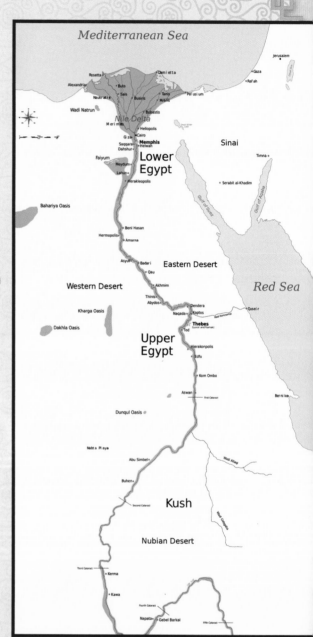

Despite their names, Lower Egypt is located north of Upper Egypt.

dangerous whitewater rapids. Only the most courageous sailors would risk these difficult waters.

Egypt's unique geography provided natural barriers on all sides against enemies. Few ventured in. The Egyptians themselves made excursions into other lands, especially in the civilization's later years. But isolated from constant warring invaders, their civilization developed almost completely undisturbed. It was not deeply influenced or changed by outside cultures in the same way other civilizations were.

Without the ongoing worry of hostile attack, the Egyptian people lived in relative peace and security. This allowed them to turn their attention to the things that mattered most: harmony within society, family, leisure pursuits, monumental building projects, and preparation for the afterlife. The result was a unique and lasting culture.

A painting from the wall of an ancient Egyptian tomb depicting people harvesting wheat by hand

Chapter 2

Rule of the
Pharaohs

The ancient Egyptians were careful record keepers. Using their unique hieroglyphic alphabet, they documented their daily life and their history. Their culture is also reflected in other remains, such as sculptures, poetry, song lyrics, and paintings. Some of the most important of these records were the long lists

of the names of pharaohs, the kings who governed during the civilization's 3,000-year history.

Many of the pharaohs' names and deeds are well known today. Others we know nothing about. But the records show that power most often passed down within a family. Over time, this created powerful ruling dynasties. This in turn generally kept society stable. Life proceeded in an expected orderly way.

The word "pharaoh" once referred to the palace of the king. An ancient Egyptian king was never addressed as "pharaoh." But by about 1185 BCE, "pharaoh" was a term often used to refer to a king.

As ruler of a united kingdom, one of the pharaoh's most important titles was "The Lord of the Two Lands." He headed both the government and the military, and he was the chief priest. But he was not looked upon as an ordinary man. Ancient Egypt was a society with deep religious roots and traditions. The king was considered a divine being, part human and part god. He was identified with the falcon god Horus. His power was absolute because the gods had authorized it.

The walls of buildings and tombs in Egypt hold stories of ancient Egyptians told through hieroglyphs, paintings, and reliefs (left). Some of these works include pharaohs interacting with the falcon god Horus (above).

The pharaoh's divinity also required him to perform important ceremonies and rituals. These rites ensured that order and balance were maintained throughout the kingdom. Everyone looked to the rulers to keep the society smooth-running and harmonious. But history shows that ancient Egypt did not always function smoothly.

Sometimes a family's power was disrupted. Then the world fell into chaos and confusion. Periods of peace were interrupted by these times of disruption. The records left by the ancient Egyptians tell the dramatic story.

The written record of ancient Egyptian history begins with the Early Dynastic period (also called the Archaic period). Beginning around 3100 BCE, the period was a time of ambitious rulers who oversaw a quickly developing civilization. Over the next 2,000 years, three major periods of stability and relative peace followed, known as the Old Kingdom, the Middle Kingdom, and the New Kingdom.

The rulers were extremely powerful during these "kingdoms," which were divided into dynasties. Society as a whole advanced. Power remained within single families, passing down from one relative to the next. But each of the kingdoms was followed by an intermediate period. These periods were times of unrest and drastic change.

The pharaoh Akhenaten (right) and Queen Nefertiti

Pyramid Builders

Some of the earliest kings were responsible for building the pyramids. In the third dynasty the high priest Imhotep designed the first pyramid, the famous step pyramid at Saqqara, for the pharaoh Djoser. Sneferu built three pyramids in the fourth dynasty (ca. 2613–2494 BCE). The pyramids at Giza are some of the most spectacular structures still in existence. Various kings built them, but Khufu, the second king of the fourth dynasty, built the largest and oldest of these. It is famously known as the Great Pyramid of Cheops, the Greek name for Khufu. The Great Pyramid is the last remaining of the Seven Wonders of the Ancient World.

The step pyramid of Djoser at Saqqara

Finally, with increasing foreign invasion, there came the Late period. During this time the native Egyptians were rapidly losing control of their land to foreign forces. But until the end of the civilization, the rule of the pharaohs was absolute.

Once a pharaoh gained the throne, he ruled for life. When he died, his son or another close male relative usually became ruler. If the pharaoh had no suitable male heir, a daughter might marry someone the family approved to be king. Sometimes a pharaoh's son and daughter would marry each other to doubly ensure power. Rarely, a female became ruler.

The most important thing was to keep control of Upper and Lower Egypt within the family. The goal was to make sure the dynasty continued over time. But when a ruling family lost power, the order of succession was lost. The big question became, "Who will rule next?"

The break in succession drove ancient Egyptian society into chaos more than once. These intermediate periods were times of turmoil and upheaval. Progress slowed, fear mounted, and war and rebellion increased.

The First Intermediate period followed the Old Kingdom. The Second Intermediate Period divided the Middle Kingdom from the New Kingdom. The Third Intermediate Period, which was the last such period, came after the New Kingdom. In all these periods, the breakdown of society came from the weakening of the pharaohs' authority. But after each intermediate period, the country was united again. New pharaohs took control. From them came new dynasties, and the birth of a new era.

The ancient Egyptians had a deep attachment to their past and its traditions. They valued order and stability. An all-powerful pharaoh symbolized an easier, more organized existence for all. So when the troubles of the intermediate periods faded away, relief spread like the Inundation. The people gladly returned to their previous way of life.

Symbols of the Pharaoh

Upper Egypt and Lower Egypt each had its own crown. Once these kingdoms were united, the pharaoh might wear either one, depending on the circumstance. On many occasions he wore the double crown, representing both lands. The crown of Upper Egypt was white. The Lower Egyptian crown was red. The double crown was a symbol of unity. It combined the two by placing the white crown into the red basket-shaped crown. Another symbol of the pharaoh is the crook and flail, which represented the king's power and role as shepherd to his people.

The flail was a whiplike device consisting of a long rod and three attached strands. The crook was a cane with a hooked handle.

The ancient Egyptians were fantastic builders and planners. And there was nothing more important to plan for than the afterlife. This was especially true for royalty. A pharaoh put much attention on preparing for his death. Above all, he needed a proper tomb.

Upon death, all royal families expected to journey to the afterlife. There they would enjoy eternal life with the gods. To prepare for the journey, useful goods such as food, beverages, furniture, and jewelry were stored in the tomb.

In the Old Kingdom (2686–2181 BCE), tombs were located beneath giant pyramids. Later the royal families began building other types of tombs and mortuary temples. Many sought to hide the whereabouts of their remains altogether. This was partly because a pharaoh's tomb held more than his mummy. It was filled with riches that attracted tomb robbers.

King Djoser built the first pyramid as a royal tomb in Saqqara in the third dynasty.

The importance of the afterlife to the ancient Egyptians is evident in the detail of the carvings and paintings in the tombs.

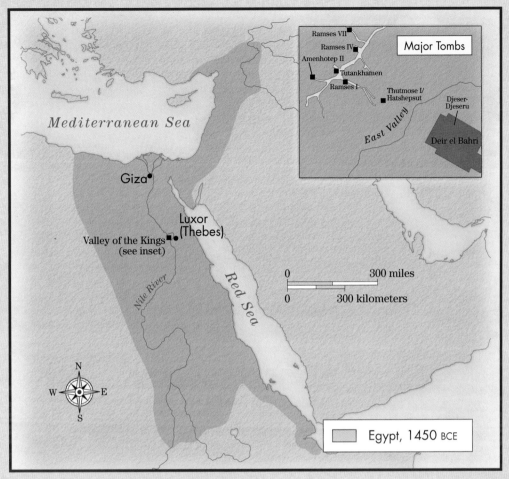

Map labels:

Major Tombs

Ramses VII
Ramses IV
Amenhotep II
Tutankhamen
Ramses I
Thutmose I/ Hatshepsut
Djeser-Djeseru
East Valley
Deir el Bahri

Mediterranean Sea

Giza

Luxor (Thebes)

Valley of the Kings (see inset)

Nile River

Red Sea

0   300 miles
0   300 kilometers

N
W E
S

Egypt, 1450 BCE

More than 60 tombs are buried in the Valley of the Kings.

Later pyramids were smooth-sided with inner shafts that plunged downward to the tombs. Originally a smooth limestone casing covered the pyramids, making them glisten under the desert sun.

During the New Kingdom (1550–1069 BCE), the pharaohs began building elaborate tombs. They chose the remote desert on the west bank of the Nile opposite the ancient city of Thebes. It seems that the first to locate his tomb there was Thutmose I. Others followed his example. Eventually so many kings were buried in the desert necropolis that it became known as the Valley of the Kings. Not far off is the Valley of the Queens, which is reported to have more than 70 tombs.

Chapter 3

Life of the People

Ancient Egyptian life was all about the family. The unit of mother, father, and children was the solid basis of a strong society. Many paintings and inscriptions on tomb walls show the loving

relationships that existed between husbands and wives, as well as between parents and children.

Many paintings show affectionate couples embracing or seated close together holding hands. Romantic love was a frequent subject in poems, songs, and other writings. All of these works are dated from the New Kingdom. One such poem includes the line, "Your hand is in my hand, my body trembles with joy, my heart is exalted because we walk together."

Marriage for the ancient Egyptians was not a religious event. It was practical. It seems to have been most important for establishing property rights. Marriages were sometimes arranged. But much evidence shows that young people were often free to choose for themselves whom to marry. Young people married early and having a large family was a common goal. Records indicate that boys usually settled down with a wife at about 16 to 20 years old. Girls often married earlier, even as soon as turning 13 or 14.

When a birth occurred, everyone was joyful. Midwives helped the mother during labor. But childhood could be a dangerous time. Nursing helped build a child's natural immunity, but the mortality rate of children was still very high. Children began eating more solid food at around 3 or 4 years old. This put them at an even higher risk because conditions were often unsanitary. Bad food could easily cause disease or even death.

Besides the simple delight of having children, it was also a practical matter for parents. History and ancestors were greatly

An ancient Egyptian painting depicts practices used in farming.

respected. Having children ensured that the family line would continue. A father usually encouraged and expected his son to carry on his profession. Starting out already having a career path made life easier for boys. And unlike some civilizations, ancient Egyptian parents valued their daughters as much as they valued their sons.

Having children was a benefit when parents got older too. Grown children had the responsibility—and the expense—of making sure their parents had a proper burial when they died. Childless couples worried about who would be there to carry out this critical task.

For the hard-working lower classes, a lifetime wasn't so long. Men lived an average of about 33 years. The average for women was even less, about 29 years. This compares to today's lifespan of 70 for men and 75 for women in Egypt.

Not surprisingly, royalty and people in society's upper class lived longer. They had better food, and more of it. They did not have to work as hard as people in the lower classes. Men normally lived into their 60s and sometimes decades longer. Upper-class women lived

The upper class of ancient Egyptian society had lavishly decorated houses.

longer too, but childbirth took a toll on all women, whether upper or lower class.

Childhood was a joyful time. Ancient Egyptian children had many kinds of toys. They played with spinning tops, balls, stone marbles, and sticks. They had dolls, usually made of clay, wood, or rags with stuffing, and doll furniture. They wrestled, raced, swam, and played various kinds of board games.

Staying clean and cool in a hot climate was important too. Young children went naked in the summer. Both boys and girls had shaved heads, except for a single ponytail-like strand that grew above one ear. The Egyptians called this the "side lock of youth."

Once children stopped nursing, they began learning how to take on adult responsibilities. The training started at a young age

The ancient game of Senet remains popular in Egypt today.

because adult life came so early. Like modern-day kids, ancient Egyptian children babysat once they had younger siblings. They learned the tasks their parents performed, according to gender. They worked in the home, in the fields, or in the places where their fathers were employed. Royalty and other wealthy families had servants who did most of this kind of work.

School was also on the agenda, at least for boys in the upper classes. Some students went to organized public schools. Others had private tutors. Most male children and some female children learned math and how to read and write. But peasant children and some girls from the upper classes did not get any official schooling. This was because they were not expected to need these abilities. But it seems clear that some ancient Egyptian women were literate. Intriguing records show that in later periods, women may have worked as scribes.

Ancient Egyptian records detail the deeds and lives of men much more than the lives of women. But it is clear that the society gave women an unusual amount of respect. They had many rights and freedoms that women in other civilizations did not have. They were even much more independent than women in later cultures, such as the Roman Empire and ancient Greece.

An Egyptian woman could inherit property, engage in lawsuits, and sue for divorce. When she married, any property she brought with her remained hers. If she divorced, she usually got between one-third and two-thirds of all the property she and her husband jointly owned. All of these were privileges women in other ancient societies generally did not have.

The Rosetta Stone

In 1799 the French army discovered the now-famous Rosetta Stone in Egypt. The stone displayed an ancient decree by the pharaoh Ptolemy V Epiphanes. The same text was written in the three scripts in use at the time: hieroglyphic, Demotic, and Greek. Widespread knowledge of Greek gave clues to the other two scripts. The scripts represented two languages, Egyptian and Greek. A young French scholar named Jean-Francois Champollion figured out how to read the hieroglyphs. The ancient world of Egypt has been dramatically revealed in part because of Champollion's brilliant puzzle-solving.

The Rosetta Stone on display at the British Museum

Chapter 4

The Role of Religion

The ancient Egyptians' spiritual life was as much a natural part of daily existence as the sun's rising and the Nile flooding its banks. It seeped into every part of life. Yet they didn't have a word for religion in their vocabulary. The science that governs the universe was almost

completely unknown in ancient times. To the Egyptians, the world operated according to the actions and whims of their gods. They worshipped numerous deities, many of which took human form. Other gods had human bodies and the heads of birds or animals. Still others had entirely animal forms.

Festivals and religious rituals were central to life. Highly honored priests guided and directed the many required rites and ceremonies. It was important to the people to follow these religious practices carefully. Doing so ensured that their human lives would reflect divine harmony.

Most of the Egyptians' religious rites were based on the lunar calendar. In some eras celebrations took place frequently. They sometimes numbered as many as 75 a year. From the time of the Old Kingdom, festivals occurred on the first, sixth, seventh, 15th, and 23rd days of each month. Most festivals were associated with a specific temple and region.

Every festival was related to something important in the life of the people. The festival might honor a sacred deity or celestial event. Some festivals celebrated events in everyday life, such as the beginning or end of harvest time. A number of annual rituals took place on the banks of the Nile. They were usually linked to the seasons.

Animal sacrifice was an important religious ritual in ancient Egypt.

A celebration honoring Apis, the Egyptian bull god

Festivals were commonly times of joyful celebration. People decorated shrines with flowers. They sang hymns and played musical instruments. They often engaged in drinking, dancing, and feasting during the festivities as well. For example, worshippers at celebrations honoring the goddess Isis did not go home empty-handed. The tens of thousands in attendance all received meat, fowl, geese, vegetables, fruits, wine, beer, oil, and more.

The celebrations and rites served to remind people of the divinity in everyday life. They helped reinforce spiritual beliefs and gave adults the opportunity to pass their wisdom down to the youth.

During important festivals people also had a chance to view their deities—in the form of statues. Most of the time, the sacred statues were kept hidden behind closed doors in dimly lit temple sanctuaries. But on certain festival occasions, the statues might be brought out for all to see. Sometimes they were carried through the streets in portable shrines. Along the way a person might have the chance to ask an oracle questions about their lives or the future.

If the festival occurred on the Nile, the deities sailed the river in flower-bedecked boats. The worshippers hailed them from the banks. But no matter the occasion or

The Great Temple of Karnak at Thebes

Times of Celebration

What: Sed Festival

When: Held during the 30th year of a pharaoh's reign,
             and then every three or four years after

Why: To celebrate the renewal of the king's physical vigor
             and magical powers

What: Beautiful Festival of the Valley

When: Held annually at the beginning of summer, lasting 12 days

Why: To celebrate the spirits of the dead

What: Festival of Opet

When: Held annually at the end of summer, lasting two to
             four weeks

Why: To celebrate the god Amun, his wife, Mut, and their
             child, Khonsu

What: Night of Tears

When: Held annually in June, at the beginning of the Inundation

Why: To celebrate the goddess Isis

Priests led a procession from a temple during the Beautiful Festival of the Valley.

its location, the time-honored rituals held the ancient Egyptians together.

Ancient Egyptian religion was centered on worship of the gods. But it also included magic and superstition. Those concepts were deeply woven into the country's religious rites and traditions. The practice of magic included spells, rituals, and amulets or other objects of supposed supernatural power.

Magic spells were used in everyday life, mostly to ward off dangers. Doctors prescribed spells along with practical medical remedies. Within the temple walls, priests and priestesses performed their own magic rituals. They also recited spells while the dead were being embalmed and during funerals.

The ancient Egyptians worshipped a long list of deities. The pharaoh in power often decided which of the deities would be considered supreme. Thus, the power among the gods sometimes

Gods and Goddesses

Deity	Role or Purpose
Horus	Falcon deity identified with the pharaoh while alive; represented by the "eye of Horus" symbol; son of Osiris and husband of Hathor
Hathor	Cow goddess of fertility; often depicted as a cow, sometimes with a human face and cow's ears
Isis	Goddess associated with nurturing and mortuary powers; associated with the life-giving qualities of the Nile; wife and sister of Osiris and mother of Horus; depicted in human form wearing a throne headdress
Osiris	God of the dead and afterlife; husband and brother of Isis; brother of Seth and father of Horus; sometimes shown in mummified form, wearing a crown and carrying a crook and flail
Seth	God of chaos and infertility and evil brother of Osiris
Re	The sun god; also known as Ra; highly important because of the Egyptians' association of the sun with life; symbolized by a shining obelisk; often appears with a hawk's or a ram's head and wearing a sun-disk headdress
Amun	Referred to as "King of the Gods"; especially powerful from the New Kingdom on; later merged with the sun god Re to become Amun-Re; often depicted in human form wearing a high, double-plumed crown or as a ram with tightly curled horns

shifted from one era to another.

Despite these changes, some gods maintained great importance through the ages. From the time of the Old Kingdom on, the king provided the royal link between the immortal deities and mere human mortals. As an intermediary, a living king was identified with the powerful god Horus, a solar deity. Horus was considered the protector of kings.

After death the pharaoh became linked to Osiris, god of the dead. Osiris was also the god of vegetation, rebirth, and the afterlife, all of which the Egyptians saw as interconnected. Because of his role presiding over funerals, Osiris was important to all people, not just the king. According to religious beliefs, the common people all expected to face Osiris after death. He had the role of judging them before they could gain safe passage into the land of the dead.

An ancient Egyptian painting of two goddesses—Isis in front and Nepthys behind her

Chapter 5

A Culture
of Riches

Living along the river in ancient Egypt meant dealing
with scorpions, snakes, wild beasts, and other threats to life.
But it was a familiar and relatively safe world. The desert on

either side, however, was a mostly uncharted danger zone. Yet in some ways, it was as essential to life as the Nile.

The deserts were not only important as burial grounds. Beneath the burning sands lay treasures, including gold, copper, amethyst, garnet, and turquoise. The precious resources were used in the building and decorating of the lavish palaces of kings. They adorned tombs and sacred temples. They brought wealth through trade.

These materials also went into the creation of a wide range of items people used every day, especially the wealthy. Some of the objects archaeologists have unearthed include furniture, decorative carvings, jewelry, hair ornaments and combs, dishware, and beautiful containers. The beauty and graceful detail of these finds show the ancient Egyptians' love of fine things and their remarkable skills as artists and craftsmen.

The homes of the upper class were full of furnishings inlaid with gold and ivory. Boats and musical instruments were built with care. Women used intricately carved jars to hold their makeup and fragrant oils.

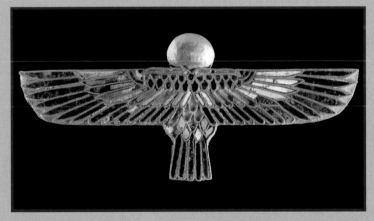

The ancient Egyptians created ornate and decorative items, such as alabaster jars (left) and gold amulets (above).

King Tut's Tomb

The world was stunned by the treasure trove of ornate items found in the tomb of Tutankhamen. When Englishman Howard Carter discovered it in 1922, the tomb contained between 3,000 and 5,000 objects.

The treasures of King Tut's tomb included two golden thrones and several other pieces of gold-covered furniture. He was buried with six chariots, multiple musical instruments, and gilded statues of gods. The archaeologist also discovered weapons, shields, fans made of gold and ostrich feathers, food, clothing, wine, and board games.

Carter found much more as well. But most spectacular was Tut's golden death mask, his solid gold coffin, and the sarcophagi encasing it. King Tut's tomb was an incredibly rare find. It was the only royal tomb in the Valley of the Kings that was nearly untouched by grave robbers.

Paintings in King Tut's tomb describe the preparations made for the afterlife.

Paintings on temple and tomb walls show the ancient Egyptians in their typical attire—simple white linen clothing. But the plain garments were like white canvasses to show off gem-studded necklaces, pendants, bracelets, and other jeweled accessories. Not all of the pieces were simply for decoration. Many of them were amulets as well, used to ward off evil and keep the wearer safe from danger or death.

Other artifacts show another aspect of ancient Egyptian life. Papyrus scrolls from ancient Egypt give a fascinating glimpse at the practice of medicine thousands of years ago. Medical treatment was far from an exact science, but the scrolls go into great detail about diagnosing disease, using medicines, and prescribing other remedies.

Medicines and herbal preparations were numerous and often made of unexpected ingredients.

Doctors used garlic, opium, castor oil, and insect and rodent parts in their remedies. These medical practitioners were good at setting broken bones. They performed dentistry and various types of surgery. They found ways to treat ailments through a combination of trial and error and pure guesswork.

Ancient Egyptian doctors also added magic to their methods. They prescribed magic potions, charms, and talismans meant to ward off illness, cure disease, or speed up healing. But if a case were serious

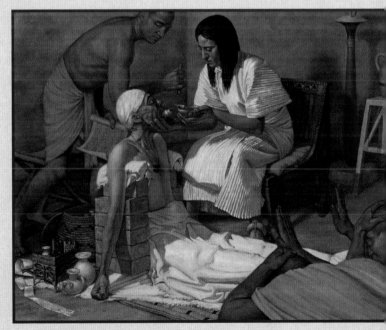

A physician uses an unusual treatment for lockjaw.

35

enough, the patient might be sent to a temple for a period of incubation. It was a time of rest in the presence of a deity. The hope was that the god would deliver a healing.

Death to the ancient Egyptians was not a frightening unknown. It was simply a passage to the next life. And having one's body properly prepared for the afterlife was an essential and sacred act. But not all Egyptians were mummified. Only royalty and the rich could afford mummification, an elaborate process.

The brain was not considered important for the afterlife. Therefore, during mummification the brain tissue was drawn out through the nostrils with a hook. This method kept the face intact. Next embalmers made an incision in the abdomen and removed the internal organs. The intestines, liver, stomach, and lungs were placed in four individual containers. The containers, called canopic jars, had lids in the shapes of four protective spirits: a jackal, a baboon, a falcon, and a human. They were known as the Four Sons of Horus.

The heart received special attention. It was carefully removed, wrapped, and placed back into the chest cavity. The Egyptians considered the heart the center of intelligence and emotion. They believed that after death, the god of death would place the heart on a scale and weigh it against a feather.

Canopic jars held internal organs.

The Egyptian belief was that a good person's heart should weigh less than the feather. So the test was meant to determine one's fate in the afterlife.

The next step in mummification was to fill the empty abdomen with a combination of fragrant spices, strips of linen cloth, and sawdust. Then the embalmers applied natron, a grayish-white mineral salt, to the body. The natron dried out the corpse, which might take two months or more. When the mummy was dry, bandaging began. Long strips of linen, sometimes in several layers, were wrapped tightly around the body, with each limb wrapped separately. Every toe and finger was also individually wrapped. The strips of linen were often soaked in resin first, to keep the bandages secure. During this wrapping process, the embalmers tucked

protective charms and amulets in between the layers of linen.

The tradition of mummification endured throughout almost all of ancient Egypt's 3,000-year history. During that time techniques changed and evolved. The art reached its peak in the New Kingdom. Then it went slowly into decline. Eventually preservation of the body became secondary to creating a fancy-looking wrapping for the corpse. In the end, bodies were just dunked in pitch or another similar substance. But these blackened mummies became so brittle that parts of the body could snap off.

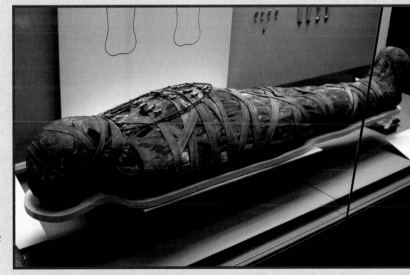

The mummification process kept bodies intact for thousands of years.

Chapter 6

End of Power

The words "ancient Egypt" bring many strong
impressions to mind. Pyramids, pharaohs, mummies, and the
Great Sphinx are only a few of the familiar images that have

endured through the ages. The imagery is still with us, but after lasting so long, why did such a strong culture die out?

When invading forces did manage to gain power in Egypt, it was almost always short-lived. And their control was usually limited to regional territories. But one group of foreign rulers brought widespread trouble to ancient Egypt: the Asiatic Hyksos. Little is known about them, but they began to gain power during the Second Intermediate Period (1650–1550 BCE).

During this era several dynasties were competing for control of the country. The Hyksos became more and more powerful, especially in parts of the south and in the eastern delta. They even managed to establish a capital in the delta city of Avaris.

Two Hyksos dynasties existed at the same time, the 15th and the 16th. Of these, the 15th was far more powerful, lasting about 100 years. But eventually the Theban kings had had enough. One after another, they began waging all-out war on the Hyksos.

The battle against the Hyksos began with Sekenenre-Tao, king of Thebes. His son Kamose continued the war after his death. Finally, Ahmose I, the son of Kamose, managed to expel the Hyksos from Avaris in the mid-1500s BCE. The Hyksos fled Egypt altogether, chased out by Ahmose's armies.

By about 1550 BCE, the Hyksos were gone and Ahmose had united the country once again. This marked the beginning of the New Kingdom. As the first pharaoh of that era, Ahmose gave a start to the mighty 18th dynasty.

The relationship between Cleopatra and Mark Antony was retold in William Shakespeare's tragedy *Antony and Cleopatra*.

Advanced Warfare

The ancient Egyptians didn't seem to be war-minded. During the Old
Kingdom, they didn't have a permanent army. Some military forces did
exist in the Middle Kingdom, mostly for fighting against the Nubians in
the south. But it was the Hyksos who proved the value of having a large
organized military. The Hyksos left their mark in another way as well.
They introduced the horse-drawn chariot into Egypt, forever changing the
ways of battle.

The Hyksos introduced a fighting style to Egypt that included
shooting arrows from horse-drawn chariots.

It was one of ancient Egypt's most outstanding and accomplished dynasties, lasting close to 250 years.

After driving out the Hyksos, the Egyptians began to realize their vulnerability. They saw their safe and isolated way of life coming to an end as other groups began invading. They became more aggressive about striking first.

During the 19th dynasty, the rulers warred continually. Their purpose was to maintain the land and power they already had. They also wanted to expand their territory. Ramses II was an army commander who became pharaoh in about 1279 BCE. He led vicious battles against the kingdom of the Hittites in what is now northern Syria.

Later, in about 1213 to 1203 BCE, Libyan forces began crossing the Egyptian borders. Other outward quests and invasions followed, including battles against troops the Egyptians called the Sea Peoples. The 20th dynasty saw Egypt's territory and influence shrinking. Rival dynasties began springing up all over. People declaring themselves king and trying to seize power was a common occurrence throughout the 21st, 22nd, and 23rd dynasties. This fractured rule weakened Egypt and led to constant upheaval and confusion.

Even in times of relative peace and unity in the 25th dynasty, an air of turmoil brewed. The Assyrians invaded in that dynasty around 671 BCE. Later the Babylonians

Ramses II led his army against the Hittites in a battle at Kadesh.

Alexander the Great was a powerful leader who conquered much of the known world at a young age.

laid siege to Egypt under King Nebuchadnezzar. But the worst of the conquerors came at the end of the 500s BCE. The power of Persia overshadowed every other civilization in the Near East. Despised by the Egyptians, the Persians stormed in and brutally took control of their land. The conquerors' rule lasted until the late 300s BCE. Then Alexander the Great quickly claimed victory over the Persians' entire widespread empire.

The Egyptians celebrated the young Macedonian king, who was then about 24 years old. Egypt was again a nation unified under one ruler. But when Alexander died in 323 BCE, he had no heir or obvious successor. Power struggles broke out yet again. In the end a Macedonian family, the Ptolemies, became the ruling dynasty in Egypt.

The Ptolemaic dynasty lasted more than 250 years. It began in

305 BCE, when Ptolemy I took the throne. The dynasty was unbroken until the death of Cleopatra VII, the last of the Ptolemies, in 30 BCE. Cleopatra took her own life, dreading the takeover of her kingdom by the Romans.

Cleopatra's death brought an end to the once great ancient Egyptian way of life. The Roman Empire was now the most dominant force in the world. It was a civilization with its own gods and ways of ruling. And though the Romans had control of Egypt, they did not adopt much of Egyptian culture.

The ancient Egyptian civilization died out more than 2,000 years ago. But its power to fascinate the world has never faded away. Egyptologists continue to discover more about it. New artifacts are continually being unearthed. New light is shed on previously found objects. New theories and interpretations replace older ones about events that occurred thousands of years ago. Egypt's past remains alive throughout the modern world. Museums around the globe contain amazing Egyptian artifacts. The pyramids and the Great Sphinx still greet visitors to their land. And the popularity of movies and books based on mummies, the pyramids, and Egypt's kings and queens never seems to wane. Clearly, the intriguing ancient Egyptian civilization has captured human imagination, and it probably always will.

Many historical documents were lost during a fire that destroyed the library of Alexandria in Egypt in 48 BCE.

Timeline

Early Dynastic Period   3100–2686 BCE   Dynasties 0 through 2

•First kings begin ruling at Memphis

Old Kingdom   2686–2181 BCE   Dynasties 3 through 6

•Step Pyramid of Djoser built at Saqqara (third dynasty)
•Great Pyramid of Khufu built at Giza (fourth through sixth dynasties)

First Intermediate Period   2181–2055 BCE   Dynasties 7 through mid-11

•Herakleopolitan rulers take power (ninth and 10th dynasties)

Middle Kingdom   2055–1650 BCE   Dynasties mid-11 through 14

•Mentuhotep II gains the throne and reunites Egypt, starting the 12th dynasty

Second Intermediate Period   1650–1550 BCE   Dynasties 15 through 17

•Hyksos begin approximately 100-year invasion

New Kingdom   1550–1069 BCE   Dynasties 18 through 20

•Ahmose drives out the Hyksos (18th dynasty)

•Thutmose III erects Hall of Records and Festival Hall at Karnak (18th dynasty)

•Prosperous temple-building period under Amenhotep III (18th dynasty)

•Akhenaten moves Egypt's capital city to Akhetaten (Tel-el-Amarna) (18th dynasty)

•Tutankhamen returns capital to Thebes (18th dynasty)

•Battle against Hittites (19th dynasty)

Third Intermediate Period   1069–747 BCE   Dynasties 21 through 24

•Rule split between Upper and Lower Egypt, with powerful priests
 governing in Upper Egypt, kings in Lower Egypt

Late Dynastic Period   747–332 BCE   Dynasties 25 through 30

•Kushite Dynasty (25th dynasty)   •First Persian Period (525–404 BCE)

•Conquest by Assyrians (25th dynasty)   •Second Persian Period (343–332 BCE)

•Assyrians destroy Thebes   •Alexander conquers Persians and
                                        takes Egypt (332 BCE)

Ptolemaic Period   332–30 BCE

•Ptolemy 1 begins new dynasty of rulers after the death of Alexander

•Cleopatra and Anthony defeated by Romans, marking the end of the Egyptian empire

Glossary

amulet—piece of jewelry carried or worn for good luck or for protection against evil

crook—long stick or staff with a curved end that was used by shepherds; along with the flail, the crook was a symbol of the pharaoh's power

delta—the flat area where a main river stream breaks up into separate, smaller channels that together form a triangular shape

Demotic—relating to a form of ancient Egyptian writing

dynasty—succession of leaders who are related to one another

Egyptologist—scientist in the field of archaeology who studies the culture of ancient Egypt

embalm—to treat a dead body using substances that protect it from decay

flail—short wood-handled tool used in ancient Egypt to separate seeds from harvested grains; along with the crook, the flail was a symbol of the pharaoh's power

hieroglyphs—system of writing that uses the picture script of ancient Egypt

intermediary—someone who acts as a go-between among various groups or a spokesperson relaying messages from one group to another

literate—able to read and write

mortuary temple—memorial temple created to honor a pharaoh's life

necropolis—large burial ground or cemetery

obelisk—enormous four-sided pillar that ends in a pyramid shape; in ancient Egypt obelisks were often inscribed with hieroglyphs

oracle—fortune-teller through whom the gods were believed to speak to mortals

papyrus—a plant that was processed and made into paperlike material for writing

resin—sticky brown or yellow substance sometimes used in adhesives

sarcophagus—heavy stone coffin, usually carved with writings honoring the deceased

talisman—good luck charm held or worn and meant to bring good fortune and ward off evil

Select Bibliography

Andreu, Guillemette. *Egypt in the Age of the Pyramids.*
David Lorton, trans. Ithaca & London: Cornell University Press, 1997.

Brewer, Douglas J., and Emily Teeter. *Egypt and the Egyptians.*
Cambridge, UK: Cambridge University Press, 2001.

Bunson, Margaret. *The Encyclopedia of Ancient Egypt.*
New York: Gramercy Books, 1991.

Egypt. The British Museum. 8 May 2012.
www.ancientegypt.co.uk/

"Egyptians." BBC History. 8 May. 2012.
www.bbc.co.uk/history/ancient/egyptians/

Heilbrunn Timeline of Art History. Metropolitan Museum of Art.
8 May 2012. www.metmuseum.org/toah/works-of-art/34.2.1

Oakes, Lorna, and Lucia Gahlin. *Ancient Egypt.*
New York: Barnes & Noble Publishing, Inc., 2006.

Strouhal, Eugene. *Life of the Ancient Egyptians.*
Norman: University of Oklahoma Press, 1992.

White, John Manchip. *Everyday Life in Ancient Egypt.*
New York: Perigee Books, 1963.

Source Note

Page 19, line 7: Douglas J. Brewer and Emily Teeter. "Ancient Egyptian Society and
Family Life." 11 May 2012. Cambridge University Press.
www.fathom.com/course/21701778/session1.html

Further Reading

Adamson, Heather. *Ancient Egypt: An Interactive History Adventure.* Mankato, Minn.: Capstone Press, 2010.

Bolton, Anne. *Pyramids and Mummies.* New York: Simon & Schuster Books for Young Readers, 2008.

Boyer, Crispin. *National Geographic Kids Everything Ancient Egypt.* Washington, D.C.: National Geographic, 2011.

Fitzgerald, Stephanie. *Ramses II: Egyptian Pharaoh, Warrior, and Builder.* Minneapolis, Minn.: Compass Point Books, 2009.

Gifford, Clive. *Food and Cooking in Ancient Egypt.* New York: PowerKids Press, 2010.

Sloan, Christopher. *Mummies: Dried, Tanned, Sealed, Drained, Frozen, Embalmed, Stuffed, Wrapped, and Smoked ... and We're Dead Serious.* Washington, D.C.: National Geographic, 2010.

Weil, Ann. *The World's Most Amazing Pyramids.* Chicago: Raintree Publishing, 2012.

Williams, Marcia. *Ancient Egypt: Tales of Gods and Pharaohs.* Somerville, Mass.: Candlewick Press, 2011.

On the Web

Use FactHound to find Internet sites related to this book. All of the sites on FactHound have been researched by our staff.

Here's all you do:

Visit www.facthound.com

Type in this code: 9780756545635

Titles in this Series:

The Byzantine Empire
Ancient China
Ancient Egypt
Ancient Greece
The Ancient Maya
Mesopotamia

Index

About the Author

Pamela Dell is the author of many nonfiction books for children and young people, including *Hatshepsut: Egypt's First Female Pharaoh*. Her other work includes a 12-book series of historical fiction and award-winning children's interactive multimedia. Pamela splits her time between Chicago and her home in Los Angeles.

The Korean War

DISCARDED

by Andrew Santella

Content Adviser: Major Peter G. Knight,
Department of History, United States Military Academy,
West Point, New York

Reading Adviser: Rosemary G. Palmer, Ph.D.,
Department of Literacy, College of Education,
Boise State University

COMPASS POINT BOOKS
MINNEAPOLIS, MINNESOTA

Compass Point Books
3109 West 50th Street, #115
Minneapolis, MN 55410

Visit Compass Point Books on the Internet at *www.compasspointbooks.com*
or e-mail your request to *custserv@compasspointbooks.com*

On the cover: With her brother on her back, a weary Korean girl tiredly trudges by a stalled M-26 tank, at Haengju, Korea, on June 9, 1951.

Photographs ©: DVIC/NARA, cover; Prints Old & Rare, back cover (far left); Library of Congress, back cover, 6, 14; The Granger Collection, New York, 5, 18, 32; Hulton-Deutsch Collection/Corbis, 7; Bettmann/Corbis, 10, 13, 25, 27, 29, 36; Howard Sochurek/Time & Life Pictures/Getty Images, 11; Corbis, 17, 24; Hulton Archive/Getty Images, 19, 35; U.S. Marine Corps/Naval Historical Foundation, 21; James Mackey, 22; AFP/Getty Images, 30; Keystone/Getty Images, 33; Central Press/Getty Images, 37; Michael S. Yamashita/Corbis, 39; KCNA via Korean News Service/AFP/Getty Images, 40; Svetlana Zhurkin, 41.

Editor: Julie Gassman
Page Production: Noumenon Creative
Photo Researcher: Svetlana Zhurkin
Cartographer: XNR Productions, Inc.
Library Consultant: Kathleen Baxter

Creative Director: Keith Griffin
Editorial Director: Carol Jones
Managing Editor: Catherine Neitge

Library of Congress Cataloging-in-Publication Data
Santella, Andrew.
  The Korean War/ by Andrew Santella
      p. cm.—(We the people)
  Includes bibliographical references and index.
  ISBN-13: 978-0-7565-2027-4 (hardcover)
  ISBN-10: 0-7565-2027-4 (hardcover)
  ISBN-13: 978-0-7565-2039-7 (paperback)
  ISBN-10: 0-7565-2039-8 (paperback)
  1. Korean War, 1950–1953—Juvenile literature. I. Title. II. We the People (Series)
(Compass Point Books)
  DS918.S25 2007
  951.904'2—dc22   2006006767

TABLE OF CONTENTS

THE WORLD SURPRISED

It was another Sunday in the middle of Korea's rainy season. In the dark hours before dawn on June 25, 1950, a steady rain fell along the border between North Korea and South Korea. Now and then, the sound of gunfire broke the quiet. But this alone was no reason for alarm. For months, North Korean and South Korean troops had been fighting in small border skirmishes. Short bursts of gunfire seemed almost as common as the rain.

But this time, the gunfire did not stop. Instead, the fighting spread to other points along the border. Heavy artillery joined in the battle. Then about 90,000 North Korean troops crossed the border into South Korea and began streaming to the south. This was no ordinary border clash. This was an invasion. North Korea had launched a massive attack on its neighbor to the south.

As more North Korean troops poured over the border, others attacked South Korea by sea. Within

4

hours, North Korea had seized the South Korean city of Kaesong. By noon, South Korea's capital city, Seoul, was under attack.

A 1950 editorial cartoon predicted the explosive result of war following the North Korean invasion of South Korea on June 25.

President Harry S. Truman

South Korea's military was caught completely unprepared. So was the country's most powerful ally, the United States. U.S. President Harry S. Truman later recalled how the invasion had shocked him. "It was a complete surprise to me, as it was to nearly everybody else even all over the world. Nobody thought any such thing would take place."

Now President Truman and other U.S. leaders faced the difficult decision of how to respond to the invasion. Should the United States rush to help defend South Korea? And if the U.S. military did join the fight, would it be able to stop the North Korean advance? In the first hours of the Korean War, there were no easy answers.

A NATION DIVIDED

North Korea and South Korea had not always been divided. In fact, the Korean peninsula had been united as a single country for centuries. Koreans called their country Choson, which means "the land of the morning calm." The country was rarely calm, however. For centuries, Korea was unable to fight off stronger countries seeking to expand their empires. China and Japan took turns invading and dominating the peninsula country. For both,

Thatched roofs covered buildings in a typical Korean town in 1910.

7

Korea served as an invasion route toward the other. Finally in 1910, Japan took control of Korea and made it part of its growing empire.

When Japan was defeated in World War II (1939–1945), its empire fell. The United States and the Soviet Union took control of lands that the Japanese had ruled. Korea was split in two. Soviet troops occupied the northern half of Korea, while U.S. troops occupied the southern half. To divide the two sections of Korea roughly in half, a U.S. official picked out a line on a map to serve as a boundary. He chose a line called the 38th parallel.

In the years after World War II, the Soviet Union and the United States were engaged in a conflict called the Cold War. The United States and its allies favored open, democratic government. The Soviet Union and its allies practiced a system of government called communism. Both the Soviets and the Americans tried to expand their power around the globe. But their rivalry did not erupt into actual fighting. Instead, the Cold War was largely a battle of words and ideas between the United States and the Soviet Union. The Soviets gave military support to other countries that set up communist governments. At the same

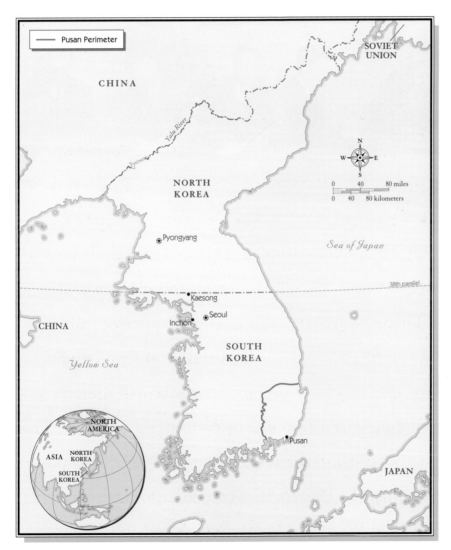

The Korean peninsula sits between China and Japan.

President Truman asked Congress for $400 million to defend the countries of Greece and Turkey from communist pressure. This request grew into the Truman Doctrine.

time, the United States and other democratic powers supported democratic governments around the world.

The United States also worked to prevent the spread of communist governments. In 1947, President Truman declared that he would provide economic and military aid to foreign nations threatened by communist takeover. This promise became known as the Truman Doctrine. It was in Korea that the United States would act on this doctrine and the Cold War would erupt into open conflict.

10

THE PATH TO WAR

The line dividing North Korea and South Korea was supposed to be temporary. Members of various Korean political parties discussed their visions for a unified Korea. However, they disagreed about the direction their country should take. Korean political leaders turned to either the United States or the Soviet Union for support. As a result, North Korea and South Korea followed different paths.

North Korean leader, Kim Il Sung (bottom, far right), was supported with a group of Soviet military advisers.

In North Korea, the Soviet occupiers made Kim Il Sung the premier and created a Soviet-style communist government called the Democratic People's Republic of Korea. To support it, they created a huge North Korean army. The Soviet Union supported the army, known as the North Korean People's Army (NKPA), by equipping it with Russian tanks and artillery.

In South Korea, national elections were held in 1948. The elections established the new Republic of Korea and made Syngman Rhee the country's first president. The United States supported the new Republic of Korea, but it did not offer the kind of military help that the Soviets offered to North Korea. The South Korean army could not match North Korea's in tanks or aircraft.

Korea remained split in two. From across the border, the governments of North Korea and South Korea viewed each other with suspicion and distrust. Some observers in other countries feared that civil war would break out in Korea. But U.S. military leaders did

South Koreans waited in long lines to vote in the nation's first election.

not believe that North Korea would invade South Korea.
In fact, the United States had removed all but about 500
troops from South Korea.

In 1949, North Korean leader Kim Il Sung secretly received permission from communist leaders in the Soviet Union and China to invade South Korea. The invasion

Kim Il Sung asked communist leaders for permission to invade South Korea during a 1949 visit to the Soviet Union.

14

began the following year. When it came, South Korea proved unready to defend itself. Of South Korea's 95,000 troops, about one-third were away from their posts on leave. The roughly 63,000 soldiers who remained were not enough to stop the NKPA invasion force of 90,000. The South Korean defense quickly crumbled.

President Truman was spending the weekend relaxing with his family at his home in Independence, Missouri, when he learned of the invasion. He rushed back to Washington, D.C., and met with his advisers to discuss the U.S. response. Some military aides advised him not to get involved in the war. Korea was halfway around the world and of little strategic value, they told him.

But Truman worried that if the United States did nothing to stop the invasion, communist powers would try to invade other countries. He wanted to show America's allies that the United States would defend democratic nations from outside interference. Truman vowed to turn back the invasion.

THE UNITED NATIONS

President Truman turned to the United Nations for help. On June 25, 1950—the same day as the invasion—the United States introduced a resolution in the United Nations Security Council. It urged members of this international peacekeeping organization to support driving the North Koreans out of South Korea. The Security Council voted 9-0 to help South Korea. That same day, Truman announced that the U.S. Air Force and Navy would support South Korea's military. He did not send troops to fight on the ground, however, because the use of ground troops was more likely to result in heavy American casualties.

The invasion continued. North Korean troops captured Seoul, South Korea's capital city. Soon nearly all of South Korea would belong to North Korea. On June 30, Truman decided to send U.S. ground troops to join the fight. He acted without asking Congress to declare war.

U.N. Security Council members raised their hands in support of the resolution to drive North Korea out of South Korea.

The U.S. Constitution gives Congress—not the president—the power to make declarations of war. But in this case, Truman used his authority as commander in chief of the military to send the troops, without ever speaking of war. In fact, even though American troops would fight and

17

The June 28, 1950, issue of The New York Times *reported the U.S. involvement in Korea.*

die in Korea for three years, Congress never made a formal declaration of war.

On July 7, the United Nations called on its members to help turn back the North Koreans. Twenty nations responded by sending combat units, medical teams, and other help to South Korea. Soldiers from all the countries would fight as part of a joint command, which was led by the United States. Truman named General Douglas MacArthur to command all the U.N. forces in South Korea. MacArthur, who had proven himself

General Douglas MacArthur

during World War I and World War II, held the highest rank given by the U.S. Army as a five-star general.

Even with the aid of other countries, the fight to help South Korea was mostly an American effort. Most of the air power, naval power, and ground forces came from the United States. But enlisting the support of the United Nations and its member nations was important. It showed that much of the world was unified in resisting the North Korean invasion.

In the first days of the war, it seemed that nothing could stop the North Koreans. The first American troops rushed into combat in Korea were inexperienced and lacked proper training. They suffered many defeats and had to retreat again and again. By early August, the North Koreans had pushed the defenders to the southeastern tip of the Korean peninsula. There the troops organized a desperate defense. They knew that retreating further would leave all of Korea in North Korea's possession.

"There will be no more retreating," U.S. General Walton Walker said. Now the U.N. defenders set up a 150-mile-long (240-kilometer) defensive line called the Pusan Perimeter. Their hope was to defend that line until more troops could arrive to reinforce them. Wherever the North Koreans attacked along the line, the U.N. defenders

Two American soldiers observed operations during the defense of the Pusan Perimeter.

rushed to meet them and push them back.

Finally, help began to arrive. Troops from Great Britain joined the fight on the U.N. side. For the first time in the war, the defenders were able to field an army as large as North Korea's. U.S. air forces took control of the skies over Korea. The success along the Pusan Perimeter gave the U.N. forces hope for the first time.

LANDING AT INCHON

General MacArthur came up with a bold plan to build on the Pusan Perimeter success. He would launch a counterattack deep behind North Korean lines. U.N. troops would travel by sea to the port city of Inchon. Although far behind the battle lines, Inchon was just 20 miles (32 km) west of Seoul. From there they could storm the beaches and begin moving inland to recapture Seoul.

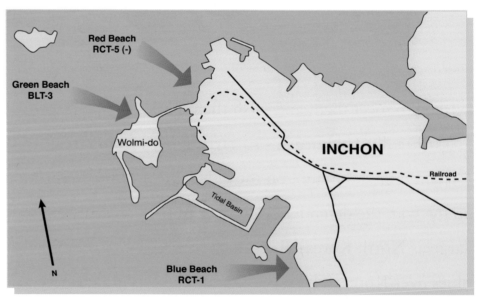

A map shows the invasion routes for the landing at Inchon.

It was a dangerous gamble. The port had several physical challenges, including a narrow entry point and violent currents, that made landing there difficult. Even some of MacArthur's generals thought the plan was a bad idea. If any part of the plan went wrong, the U.N. troops could easily be wiped out. But MacArthur insisted the plan would work. "We shall land at Inchon, and I shall crush them," he promised.

On September 13, U.S. and British destroyer ships began firing on North Korean positions near Inchon. The attack was so intense that it left many North Korean defenders ready to surrender.

Then early on September 15, hundreds of U.S. and British ships began carrying more than 70,000 U.S. Marines and other U.N. troops toward the shore at Inchon. Landing crafts carried the Marines to the beaches, and from there they rushed ashore. Some troops used ladders to scale the high concrete walls that protected parts of Inchon from the sea. Some attacked North Korean machine gun

U.S. and British ships sped toward the beaches of Inchon.

nests. In some cases, they found the North Koreans waiting with their arms raised in surrender.

MacArthur's plan worked perfectly. As the Marines moved ashore, ships carried tanks, bulldozers, and other equipment to the beaches to support them. North Koreans put up a weak resistance. Within hours, the U.N. forces had taken Inchon, captured hundreds of prisoners, and suffered light casualties. Within two weeks, they had pushed the North Koreans out of Seoul and sent them into full retreat. By October, the North Koreans had been driven back across the 38th parallel. MacArthur's risky plan had turned the tide of the war. Finally, the North Koreans were on the defensive.

This success left the U.N. forces with a difficult decision: Should they pursue the NKPA north past the 38th parallel and into North Korea? Or was their mission

Debris filled the streets of Seoul in early October 1950.

complete now that the North Koreans had been driven out of South Korea? South Korean president Syngman Rhee wanted the U.N. forces to keep fighting and to create "one Korea." Truman agreed, and the U.N. Security Council supported this decision in a resolution passed on October 7. U.N. forces invaded North Korea and captured more territory. On October 19, they took North Korea's capital, Pyongyang.

These new developments worried China's leader, Mao Tse-tung. As the head of a communist power, he did not like seeing U.N. troops rolling through North Korea. He feared they might even attack China itself. Mao ordered Chinese troops to mass along the Yalu River, which forms the border between China and North Korea.

Late in October, the Chinese army, known as the Chinese Communist Forces (CCF), began moving over the border into North Korea. The Chinese battled American and U.N. troops for the first time on October 25. The Chinese scored a victory, paused, and faded back into the

26

mountains of North Korea as quickly as they had emerged. MacArthur was reassured by the retreat. With Truman's full approval, he launched another attack. But the CCF fought back in overwhelming numbers. The Americans and other U.N. forces found themselves retreating again. "We face an entirely new war," General MacArthur said.

More than 10,000 Seoul citizens gathered to protest the Chinese involvement in the Korean War.

THE NEW WAR

American and U.N. troops faced a terrible challenge. The Chinese fielded a huge army of 300,000 soldiers. They fought fiercely and attacked in waves that never seemed to let up—no matter how many casualties they suffered. As they advanced, they often blew whistles and bugles to signal to each other. U.N. troops came to dread the noise that went along with the deadly Chinese attacks.

The U.N. forces also had to deal with a brutal Korean winter. Bitterly cold weather made it difficult to march, sleep, or even eat. One Marine sergeant later remembered how bare hands would freeze onto the steel weapons. Others recalled snow and ice freezing on their faces as they marched, sometimes even freezing their mouths shut. U.S. troops fought bravely as they retreated south.

As the retreat continued, thousands of Korean refugees followed behind the troops. These ordinary Koreans were trying to avoid the destruction and danger

U.S. Marines endured Korea's subzero winter temperatures.

of the war. But Communist forces sometimes dressed like civilians to blend into the population to both avoid and carry out attacks. Before this war, American troops had never faced such guerrilla tactics. It was often difficult for soldiers to tell if they were encountering the enemy or innocent civilians.

Korean refugees fled past frozen rice fields in their journey south.

By January 1951, the Chinese had recaptured all of North Korea and part of South Korea, including Seoul. The U.N. forces fought back, and both sides suffered terrible casualties. Meanwhile, American leaders began to disagree about the conduct of the war. General MacArthur thought it was time to take the war to China. He wanted permission to bomb the communist country. But President Truman believed that the war should be fought only in Korea. "We are trying to prevent a third world war," he said. The president feared attacking China could mark the start of World War III.

MacArthur openly disagreed with the president. He feared that Truman would let the war end with the two sides right back where they were when the conflict started. MacArthur wanted a clear-cut victory. He believed that his troops had fought and died for nothing less. He even did his best to break up Truman's efforts at peace talks. In March, MacArthur publicly threatened the Chinese with a full-scale war. He also questioned the ability of the Chinese army to defend China.

While MacArthur was speaking out against China, Truman was trying to arrange peace talks with the communist country. But MacArthur's tough talk angered the Chinese and hurt the opportunity for peace talks. His

31

statements also undermined the president's authority.

Finally, Truman had enough. On April 11, the president announced that he had relieved MacArthur of his command "so that there would be no doubt or confusion as to the real purpose and aim of our policy." Truman knew that the U.S. military had to accept his leadership and

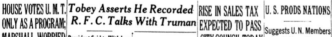

100TH ANNIVERSARY
"All the News
That's Fit to Print"
1851   1951

The New York Times.

LATE CITY EDITION

Copyright, 1951, by The New York Times Company.

VOL. C. No. 34,045.   NEW YORK, WEDNESDAY, APRIL 11, 1951.   RAG PAPER EDITION

TRUMAN RELIEVES M'ARTHUR OF ALL HIS POSTS; FINDS HIM UNABLE TO BACK U.S.-U.N. POLICIES; RIDGWAY NAMED TO FAR EASTERN COMMANDS

HOUSE VOTES U.M.T. ONLY AS A PROGRAM; MARSHALL WORRIED

Chamber Accepts Compromise Setting Up Commission to Draft Details of Plan

FUTURE LAW IS REQUIRED

Congress' Approval Is Needed to Start Universal Training— General Sees Risk in This

By JOHN D. MORRIS

WASHINGTON, April 10—Concessions offered by advocates of Universal Military Training to save the program from outright rejection were approved today by the House of Representatives, but it remained to be seen whether the aim had been achieved.

General of the Army George C. Marshall, Secretary of Defense, meanwhile voiced the fear that current maneuvering in the House might "largely emasculate" the training features of the pending draft and training bill.

It was not clear, however, whether he was concerned over the main fight, expected later this week, over a proposal to eliminate all Universal Military Training provisions from the bill.

It was to head this off that the

Tobey Asserts He Recorded R.F.C. Talks With Truman

President Said to Withdraw Fee Accusation—Niles Held Attempting to Aid Dawson

By C. P. TRUSSELL

WASHINGTON, April 10—Senator Charles W. Tobey, Republican of New Hampshire, was represented tonight as having told the Senate (Fulbright) subcommittee investigating the Reconstruction Finance Corporation that President Truman had charged in a telephone conversation with him that members of Congress had accepted fees for obtaining R.F.C. loans for constituents.

The Senator also was said to have reported also that in a later telephonic communication the President had said that he had been mistaken.

Both telephonic conversations were said to have been recorded on disks in Mr. Tobey's possession. The date, or dates, were not made public. The Senator declined to discuss the matter and members of the investigating group also were silent.

In another development in the R.F.C. inquiry, former Senator Burton K. Wheeler, Democrat of

Burton K. Wheeler
Associated Press

Montana, said today that he had asked Senator Tobey to "go easy on" Donald S. Dawson, White House aide, during the Senate investigation of the agency. Mr. Wheeler asserted that he acted as

Continued on Page 23, Column 3

Sterling Hayden Was a Red; 'Stupidest Thing I Ever Did'

RISE IN SALES TAX EXPECTED TO PASS CITY COUNCIL TODAY

Finance Committee Studies Bill at Length—Fight Against Measure Goes On

RUML A FISCAL ADVISER

Mayor Declines Challenge to Debate With Hoving—Joseph Suggests State-Wide Levy

The finance committee of the City Council spent an inconclusive three-hour executive session at City Hall yesterday afternoon weighing the merits of the proposed increase in the retail sales tax from 2 to 3 per cent, but when the meeting ended nothing had changed the prospect that the tax rise would be approved.

It was indicated that today the committee, after further behind-closed-doors deliberations, would favor the sales impost rise by a vote of 8 to 2, or possibly 7 to 3, and that later today the full City Council would adopt the measure by something like 19 to 6.

If the tax bill clears the Council hurdles today, as is indicated, it is expected that the Board of Estimate, whose members are committed to it, will give its approval at tomorrow's regular meeting.

U.S. PRODS NATIONS

Suggests U.N. Members Send More Troops to Fight in Korea

3 AVENUES ARE LISTED

Contributions Sought From Nations Not Yet Committed

By A. M. ROSENTHAL

UNITED NATIONS, N.Y., April 10—The United States has been quietly suggesting that members of the United Nations increase, or at least maintain, their contributions of troops for the Korean war effort.

Informed sources here report that for some time the United States has been keeping in touch with members of the world organization to see if non-United States representation in the international army could be increased.

[Chinese Communist troops in Korea clung to their positions along the Hwachon Reservoir in the face of daylong United Nations attacks. Eighth Army headquarters clamped a stringent security blackout on news from the front as a major battle seemed to impend in the reservoir area.]

DISMISSED BY THE PRESIDENT

General of the Army Douglas MacArthur

Britain Asks That Red China Have Role in Japanese Pact

PRESIDENT MOVES

Van Fleet Is Named to Command 8th Army in Drastic Shift

VIOLATIONS ARE CITED

White House Statement Quotes Directives and Implies Breaches

Texts of statements and orders in MacArthur dispute, Page 4.

By W. H. LAWRENCE

WASHINGTON, Wednesday, April 11—President Truman early today relieved General of the Army Douglas MacArthur of all his commands in the Far East and appointed Lieut. Gen. Matthew B. Ridgway as his successor.

The President said he had relieved General MacArthur "with deep regret" because he had concluded that the Far Eastern Commander "is unable to give his wholehearted support to the policies of the United States Government and of the United Nations in matters pertaining to his official duties.

General MacArthur, in a message to House Minority Lea-

The New York Times *reported the news of MacArthur's dismissal.*

follow only his plan.

Truman was widely criticized for his decision to fire the general. MacArthur returned to the United States and received a hero's welcome from cheering crowds. Truman responded that "the cause of world peace is more important than any individual."

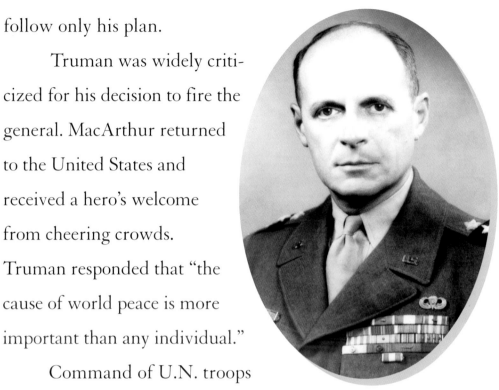

General Matthew Ridgway

Command of U.N. troops fell to General Matthew Ridgway. Ridgway was a capable leader. A month earlier he had led a group of U.N. troops in recapturing Seoul. This was the fourth and final time the city changed hands during the war.

PEACE TALKS

By summer 1951, Korea was a landscape of barbed wire and trenches. Both the countryside and the cities were badly damaged by bombardments. Finally, the two sides agreed to begin truce talks on July 10. But both sides remained distrustful, and little progress was made toward peace. Meanwhile, the fighting and killing continued on the front lines.

The main conflict in the peace talks was over the return of prisoners of war. The communist nations insisted that all Chinese and North Korean soldiers who had been captured by the United Nations must be returned when the fighting ended. But the United States argued that many Chinese and North Korean soldiers did not want to return to their home countries.

U.S. leaders claimed that these soldiers did not want to go back to countries where they would not have political freedom. "We will not buy an armistice by turning over human beings for slaughter and slavery," Truman said. The war continued for another 18 months. During that time, 9,000 U.S. soldiers lost their lives.

In April 1953, the two sides agreed to exchange sick and wounded prisoners. Not long after this, they agreed that no prisoner of war would be forced to return to his home country against his will. Any prisoner who

North Korean prisoners of war made baskets in a South Korean prison.

American troops celebrated after hearing news of the cease-fire.

did not want to return home would be granted asylum in
another country.

A cease-fire was declared to end the fighting on
July 27, 1953. More than three years had passed since the
war started. Much of the Korean peninsula was left in ruins.
Thousands of Koreans were left homeless. More than

1 million South Korean and an unknown number of North Korean civilians died as a result of the war. U.S. military personnel losses were high, with more than 33,665 soldiers dying.

U.N. forces eventually returned 75,823 prisoners to China and North Korea. The communist forces returned 12,773 American, South Korean, and U. N. prisoners.

The United Nations and communist forces exchanged groups of prisoners on August 11, 1953, in Panmunjom, Korea.

37

More than 21,000 prisoners from the communist countries chose not to return home, while only 347 U.N. prisoners elected not to return home.

Korea remained divided. In fact, at war's end, each side controlled almost the same territory it held at the start of the war. South Korea ended up gaining a small area of about 1,500 square miles (3,900 square km).

Korea is still divided today. A heavily fortified border runs between the two countries near the 38th parallel. A 2½-mile-wide (4-km) demilitarized zone (DMZ) extends all along the border. Military forces and operations are banned from this area, which is designed to keep the armies of the two nations apart.

North and South Korea have followed very different paths in the years since the war. South Korea is a stable democracy with a strong economy. It remains an ally of the United States.

In contrast, North Korea has suffered under the dictatorships of Kim Il Sung and his son Kim Jong Il.

Small rocks are placed on the fence of the demilitarized zone that separates North and South Korea. The rocks serve as an indication of passage attempts.

In the late 1990s, 2.5 million North Koreans died from famine. The country has continued to suffer severe food shortages, and many of its poorest people enjoy little political freedom or hope for improvement.

Despite these problems, North Korea has one of the largest militaries in the world, with more than 1 million

39

soldiers in the army. Also, North Korea's leaders are working to develop nuclear weapons— among the most powerful and deadly weapons in the world. This alarms leaders in the United States and other countries. They don't trust North Korea's leaders with the power that goes along with such weapons.

North Korean leader Kim Jong Il

The Korean War is sometimes called the Forgotten War. It is often overshadowed in history books by World War II, the bloodiest war in history, and the Vietnam War, a controversial conflict that the United States lost. To honor the sacrifices of Americans who fought in the

Korean War, the National Park Service opened the Korean War Veterans Memorial in Washington, D.C., in 1995. Millions of people visit the memorial each year. By educating visitors about the war, the memorial helps ensure that the Korean War will no longer be a forgotten war.

The Korean War Memorial includes life-size statues of 19 ground soldiers, ready for battle.

41

GLOSSARY

artillery—large guns, such as cannons, that require several soldiers to load, aim, and fire

asylum—protection given to refugees from another country

casualties—soldiers killed, captured, or injured during a war

civilians—people not part of a military force

communism—a system in which goods and property are owned by the government and shared in common

controversial—causing dispute or disagreement

guerrilla tactics—warfare using small, surprise attacks rather than large battles

landing crafts—boats used to bring troops ashore from larger ships

parallel—an imaginary numbered circle on Earth's surface that marks the distance north or south of the equator

skirmishes—small battles

DID YOU KNOW?

- The Korean War marked the first use of Mobile Army Surgical Hospitals, or MASH units. In MASH units, soldiers wounded in the war were given medical care very close to the front lines.

- The war became an issue in the 1952 presidential race between Republican Dwight D. Eisenhower and Democrat Adlai Stevenson. Eisenhower vowed to travel to Korea personally to look for a way to end the war. He was elected president in November 1952 and went to Korea to meet with American troops for three days the following year.

- The Korean War Veterans Memorial in Washington, D.C., depicts 19 members of U.S. armed forces on patrol in Korea. The inscription reads: "Our nation honors her sons and daughters who answered the call to defend a country they never knew and a people they never met."

- The Korean Demilitarized Zone (DMZ) contains approximately 1 million land mines, highly explosive devices buried just underground. It is one of the most heavily mined areas on Earth.

IMPORTANT DATES

Timeline

1945 Korea is split into U.S. and Soviet zones.

1948 On August 12, the Republic of Korea (South Korea) is formed; on September 9, the Democratic People's Republic of Korea (North Korea) is formed.

1950 On June 25, North Korea invades South Korea; on June 30, President Harry S. Truman orders U.S. ground forces to defend South Korea; on September 15, U.N. troops capture Inchon; on October 14, Chinese troops enter North Korea.

1951 In January, communist forces recapture Seoul; on March 18, U.N. troops retake Seoul; in July, peace talks begin.

1952 Peace talks stop because of disagreements over prisoners of war.

1953 Cease-fire agreement brings an end to Korean War.

IMPORTANT PEOPLE

KIM IL SUNG (1912–1994)

*First premier of the Democratic People's Republic of Korea
(North Korea); as a dictator, he tightly controlled many parts of
North Korean society*

DOUGLAS MACARTHUR (1880–1964)

*General who commanded U.N. forces in Korea until President
Truman removed him from command; he led troops in the landing
at Inchon, which helped turn the tide of the war*

MAO TSE-TUNG (1893–1976)

*Founder of the People's Republic of China who sent Chinese troops to
Korea in support of the North Korean People's Army*

SYNGMAN RHEE (1875–1965)

*First president of the Republic of Korea (South Korea); as an anti-
communist, he had a strong desire to unite Korea as a democracy*

HARRY S. TRUMAN (1884–1972)

*Thirty-third president of the United States; he involved U.S. troops in
the Korean War and asked members of the United Nations for support*

WANT TO KNOW MORE?

At the Library

Ashabranner, Brent K. *Remembering Korea: The Korean War Veterans Memorial.* Brookfield, Conn.: Twenty-First Century Books, 2001.

Cannarella, Deborah. *Harry S. Truman.* Minneapolis: Compass Point Books, 2003.

Feldman, Ruth Tenzer. *The Korean War.* Minneapolis: Lerner Publications Co., 2004.

Stein, R. Conrad. *The Korean War Veterans Memorial.* New York: Children's Press, 2002.

On the Web

For more information on *The Korean War*, use FactHound
to track down Web sites related to this book.

1. Go to *www.facthound.com*

2. Type in a search word related to this book
   or this book ID: 0756520274

3. Click on the *Fetch It* button.

Your trusty FactHound will fetch the best Web sites for you!

On the Road

Korean War Veterans National Museum & Library

1007 Pacesetter Drive

Rantoul, IL 61866

888/295-7212

Books, manuscripts, maps, photographs, and military and civilian documents associated with the Korean War

The Korean War Veterans Memorial

900 Ohio Drive SW

Washington, DC 20024

202/426-6841

National memorial dedicated to the soldiers who fought in the Korean War

Look for more We the People books about this era:

The 19th Amendment
ISBN 0-7565-1260-3

The Berlin Airlift
ISBN 0-7565-2024-X

The Dust Bowl
ISBN 0-7565-0837-1

Ellis Island
ISBN 0-7565-0302-7

The Great Depression
ISBN 0-7565-0152-0

Navajo Code Talkers
ISBN 0-7565-0611-5

Pearl Harbor
ISBN 0-7565-0680-8

The Persian Gulf War
ISBN 0-7565-0612-3

September 11
ISBN 0-7565-2029-0

The Sinking of the USS Indianapolis
ISBN 0-7565-2031-2

The Statue of Liberty
ISBN 0-7565-0100-8

The Titanic
ISBN 0-7565-0614-X

The Tuskegee Airmen
ISBN 0-7565-0683-2

Vietnam Veterans Memorial
ISBN 0-7565-2032-0

A complete list of We the People titles is available on our Web site:
www.compasspointbooks.com

INDEX

About the Author

Andrew Santella writes for magazines and newspapers, including *GQ* and the *New York Times Book Review*. He is the author of a number of books for young readers. He lives outside Chicago with his wife and son.